A Way Through

Grief

ELISABETH RUNDLE

Hunt & Thorpe

Tears —
pouring, choking, blinding tears.
   My world fallen apart.
I seem to be only half living...
numbly existing...
   part of me has died.
My Lord and my God,
   I am crushed by my loss
even though my heart tells me
   death is not the end.

And I heard
a loud voice from the throne saying:
"Now the dwelling of God is with men,
and He will live with them...
He will wipe every tear from their eyes.
There will be no more death or mourning
or crying or pain,
for the old order of things has passed away".

REVELATION 21:2–4

Into Thy hands... My God! My God!
In this awful hour you seem a long way off...
My whole soul is clouded by the dread mystery
of pain and death...
I thought there would be victory,
a rescue for your faithful child, and there is not.
It looks as though You had forsaken me,
as though my ultimate trust was betrayed.
Even so, I accept it.
You and Your purposes matter.
Into Your hands I commend my spirit...

EVELYN UNDERHILL

Christ leads me through no darker rooms
    Than He went through before;
And all who enter into God's eternal grace
    Must enter by this door.

My knowledge of that life is small,
    My eye of faith is dim;
But it's enough that Christ knows all,
    And we shall be with Him.

RICHARD BAXTER, adapted by the author

I suppose its only natural, Lord,
that on losing someone so close to us,
we feel lost for a long time...
help me to get through the days
just one hour at a time.
I can't focus on tomorrow
or next week or next month...
just your strength to enable me
to meet the next sympathising person
and the necessary jobs
which must be done.

Jesus said:
"Do not let your hearts be troubled,
Trust in God, trust also in me."
1 JOHN 14:1

I do trust, Lord,
though my heart is breaking...

O God,
our only help in time of need,
be close to me in my sorrow,
in Your mercy give me strength
to keep going,
and help me to trust You
whatever happens.

ETTA GULLICK

Just when I think
there are no more tears left to cry
a word, a tune, a thought...
and they stream down my face.
Nothing can take away my precious memories.
Lord, thank You for these memories —
I know I can't go on living in the past,
but right now, I can't even think ahead
during this day, let alone for the future.
I'm on automatic pilot...
help me... hold me...
take control.

Today your heart is heavy
    with sorrow and grief,
But as days turn to months
May you find sweet relief
    in knowing your loved one
Is not far away,
But is with you in spirit
Every hour of the day.

HELEN STEINER RICE

The souls
of the just are in God's hand...
they are at peace...
they will receive great blessings
because God has tested them and
found them worthy to be His.

WISDOM 3:1–5

Lord,
I feel I want to hide away...
I can't face people
and yet I'm desperate for comfort.
I need that hand on my arm,
someone just to sit there
and break this terrible silence.
I didn't realise parting brought
such paralyzing pain...

You do not give as the world gives,
O Lover of Souls.
What you give you do not take away,
for what is yours is ours also if we are yours.

And life is eternal and love is immortal,
and death is only a horizon, and a horizon is
nothing save the limit of our sight.
Lift us up, strong Son of God,
that we may see further;
cleanse our eyes that we may see more clearly:
draw us closer to yourself
that we may know ourselves
to be nearer to our loved ones
who are with you.

A prayer of FR. BEDE JARRET, adapted by Peter Barber

Lord,
You promised You would not leave
Your followers without comfort.
Please, please let me feel
Your presence, Your peace...
be to me what I need at this moment.

Peace I leave with you;
My peace I give to you;
not as the world gives,
do I give to you.
Let not your heart be troubled,
nor let it be fearful.

JOHN 14:27

Lord,
I'm being so selfish
in my misery.
I feel I'm the only person bowed in misery
but of course I'm not.
Help me to raise my eyes beyond myself
and try to comfort others who feel
equally desolate and bewildered.
May we find comfort in each other
and in our weakness
find Your strength.

May we, whenever tempted to dejection,
Strongly recapture thoughts of resurrection.
You gave us Jesus to defeat our sadness
    With Easter gladness.
Lord, you can lift us from the grave of sorrow;
Give to your people for the day's affliction
    Your benediction.

FRED KAAN

Lord, I believe.
Help my trembling, my doubts, my unbelief.
I do believe that nothing can separate me
from Love: love of my loved one, love of my loved
one and Your love. We are indissoluble
as warmth and light from a fire.
And life goes on...

I long for household voices gone,
For vanished smiles I long;
But God has led my dear one on
And He can do no wrong.

I know not what the future holds
Of marvel or surprise,
Assured alone that life and death
His mercy underlies.

JOHN GREENLEAF WHITTIER

St. Paul wrote to the Corinthians:
What you sow does not come to life unless it dies.
When you sow, you do not plant the body that will be,
but just the seed...
So it will be with the resurrection of the dead.
The body that is sown is perishable,
it is raised imperishable —
it is sown a natural body,
it is raised a spiritual body.
I CORINTHIANS 15:36–42

Yes,
Thank You Lord, for the life I loved
and for the way that life is immortalised
in my love and my life.
Direct *my* path until in Your perfect time,
we share the everlasting love
of Your eternity.

All the pain and grief is over
Every restless tossing past —
I am now at peace for ever
Safe home in heaven at last.

Jesus came Himself to meet me
Along the way so hard to tread:
And with His strong arm to lean on
There was no doubt nor dread.

Then you must not grieve so sorely
For I love you dearly still.
Try to look beyond earth's shadows
Pray to trust our Father's will.

ANON

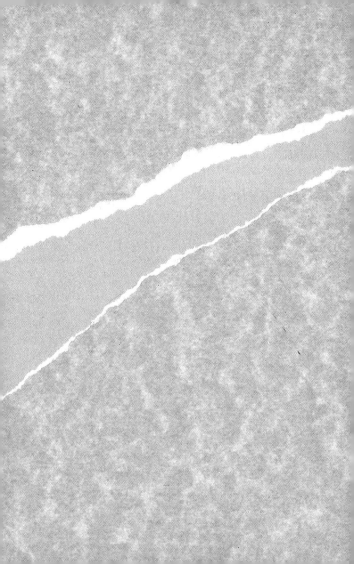

I know
that my Redeemer
lives!

JOB 19:25

Copyright © 1991 Hunt and Thorpe
Original text © Elisabeth Rundle
First published in 1991 by Hunt and Thorpe
66 High Street, Alton, Hants GU34 1ET
ISBN 1 85608 036 6

Design by Tony Cantale Graphics
Illustrations by Elvira Dadd

Manufactured in Singapore.